Ramanujan

Amit Chaudhuri

Ramanujan

Shearsman Books

First published in the United Kingdom in 2021 by
Shearsman Books
P O Box 4239
Swindon
SN3 9FN

Shearsman Books Ltd Registered Office
30–31 St. James Place, Mangotsfield, Bristol BS16 9JB
(this address not for correspondence)

www.shearsman.com

ISBN 978-1-84861-738-4

ACKNOWLEDGEMENTS
'Ramanujan' and 'Cambridge' first appeared in *Granta* online.
'Mother' appeared in *Poetry at Sangam*.

Contents

Four

Five

Six

One

Ramanujan

Mahesh would cycle or simply stride
to the Broad Street Wimpy's
to get himself a beanburger.
With a wisdom not expected
of a Tamil Brahmin from Delhi
he claimed it would suffice.
In Balliol, the alternative
was jewelled Brussels sprouts and carrots
in remnants of lukewarm water.
On good days, they – the vegetarians –
might stumble upon sauerkraut
or steaming cauliflower au gratin.
You, Heeraman, chose
to forage weekly up the Cowley Road
for turmeric, rice, and chick peas
and potent jars of chana masala powder.
In the Co-op, you'd spotted 'yoghurt'.
It was chick peas that kept you alive.
In hall, you scrutinised the mash.
Poor Ramanujan! Seventy years
before you he must have been
the first meat-abhorring Hindu
to conjure up from odds and ends
– no spices then in Oxbridge, no
curry leaves, hardly anything
even for ordinary Englishmen
in a time of conflict and rationing –
a semblance, at odd hours of night and day,
of an aroma that half-pacified
the voice that asked, *Why are you here?*

Cambridge

It took us a few days after we arrived
in the suburban flat
from which Churchill College was a glimpse away
– milk left in the fridge
by an invisible hand,
bread and jam placed recently on a kitchen shelf –
to realise Cambridge was not Oxford.
It felt more beautiful for a day.
On Madingley Road, the weather
was wet, the wind
cutting.
            Unexpectedly, the fens
became an invisible presence for us.

Then, to phrase it dramatically,
I was told I might die. I'd never felt
more well or alive (mentally,
I'd never been as out of place as in Cambridge).
From Addenbrooke's, they sent me to Papworth.

How numb we were on the eve of departure!
The journey, twenty minutes by taxi,
seemed to go on into the narrow-laned
mordant hush of a Cambridgeshire
without industry or migration: just glum stillness.
Here, past a roundabout, in a verdant
nothing, a lease of life was enforced on me.

Papworth Everard! I'd forgotten
the second, almost Gallic, half of the name.
Nothing to define it as an English village

except one Cost-Cutter.
                    Papworth.

That was the inaugural tour. The name
would keep coming up. A few days to go,
our umbrellas drenched, heavy of foot
on Madingley Road – a taxi stopped
as if the oracle had spoken: 'Do you know
the way to Papworth?' It was too much.
Defeated, we asked him to turn the car around.

Ancient wide building, the catacombs
coursing through it like veins! You and my parents
hovering at doorways, or standing, summer's ghosts,
by the curtain to my bed in the ward.
The imperial fixtures of bathtub and basin,
the unremarkable generosity of space,
and, outside, sunlight. It had stopped raining!
Despite my wakefulness that night
when I lay listening

to the woman with the smoker's rasp
remonstrating with staff recurrently,
then fell asleep, urging the dawn
to come, so I could see you
and my parents
before they took me,
despite being paraded round on a wheelchair
like a middle-aged woman in a sari
in an airport
now to X-ray, now sonography,
despite the affection I developed
for the two transplant patients who bookended my stay,
I never felt I knew the place.

I thought of Ramanujan
and the men for whom this dour house was built,
a last stop, in which the chilly breeze
through the window was therapy.
Others would sit tinkering, or daydreaming vacantly –
but Ramanujan, your spirit left your body
many times in Cambridgeshire before you went home.

Now, eighteen years after
returning one tentative afternoon
to the flat in Benian's Court,
I think of Ramanujan
where I left him in Papworth,
the war ebbing, my life beginning.
I think of you too, and my parents.

That building, unsmiling memorial
to men permanently at a loose end
among whom he was strange
misfit: what will happen to it now?

Two

God

I listen for it
in my sleepstruck daze
in the toilet.
I know it'll be there
like a greeting
meant for no one else.
It's my acknowledgement
of the day
when it's taking form.
Loudspeakers demarcate the invisible
neighbourhoods, voices
orchestral, three bodiless
muezzins floating angrily
over the beaten dun-coloured
balconies
of Park Circus and Broad Street
in a web of notes.
You forget there's no other noise.

Today I heard it
in the afternoon – when,
on Sunday, these localities start
to retreat from slumber.
I like the low growl
which itself is half-asleep.
Though it's in my proximity
it echoes from
the horizon of new buildings and old.

I've heard it up close
where the minaret and the middle-class lane
each pretend

the other cannot possibly exist.
In five bursts, ephemerally
but recurrently, a familiar memory:
the voice
so inhabits the ear
as an admonition
you have to shut the window; it's
full frontal din, impossible
to make sense of at close quarters.
It's as if human and God were face to face,
touching noses;
difficult to delineate features
and do much else but breathe His odour.
Yet those who live without the benefit of distance
apparently don't hear it at all.

From Nakhoda Masjid

The minarets
of Nakhoda mosque
tower over the lane –
a radio station
broadcasting from eternity.
Not far away, the Royal,
overlooking human and animal
traffic on Chitpur Road,
is still renowned for biriyani.

Maybe unduly so, since
the taste is nothing special.
On the first-floor balcony, we,
hands washed, examine
the restless concourse
like we were recent lovers
and not married for fifteen years.
The one remarkable feature,
besides the potato, are
the grains of rice, some
fat, unimpeachable white,
others a soiled modest yellow,
each unable to merge
with the other, crowded
in a neighbourly mass, yet polarised.
It's as if the atoms
married to make up space
had become visible separately,
some pure, unstained by light,
others heavy and radiant.

Cathedral

Not yet out of Bangalore,
muttering, 'Srirangapatna!'
we glance at our watches
but want a cup of coffee.
I'm sleepy. It's quiet inside.
Old Airport Road is far away.
A man in a suit takes us in hand.
Not a cup, it's
a tumbler of brew that's spilled
into the bowl it nestles in.
Anand Bhavan.
A cathedral.
Whatever we see later – fort
or summer palace or tomb –
no mausoleum can vie
with this hive of chairs and tables.
We're doused by the coffee's perfume.
Blue and yellow letters
balloon-like float:
'High Class Veg Indian Restaurant'.
Yet it's much more.
If Las Vegas were a cluster
of sweet and snack shops... Banana chips
pale as coins;
the ladies' fingers chips
teem, an infestation.
The place has the bored expectancy
dens have before play's begun.
In jukebox-like counters,
chandrakala and Bombay Halwa
and other families

of edible substances
glint like jackpot
in a slot machine.

Soon we're off to Srirangapatna again.

Hamburger

Not even students dare enter
the Campus Kitchen
– once known as Zest –
after 7.45.
Nothing's left –
the salads have vanished,
various species of vegetarian purée
fill large bowls on display.
There are no diners but
a resilient Chinese youth
an Arab man
and a woman in a hijab.
No, there's a tiny English girl
flicking pictures off her smartphone.
The hamburger's been joined together
without much calculation, not with the grace
of an equation, but as if creation
were simply an act of addition.
There's a bun on top,
another below,
much like one had conceptualised a mouth
without having thought up a face.
In between, naked, no longer raw, is a tongue.
There's little to do with this mouth but
eat it – it has a taste separate
from your own cheeks and flesh. You're conscious
of not devouring yourself. You add burger sauce
from what appear like bottles of paint.
The chips you dip like swollen fingers
into the guacamole.
You're hungry – hungrier than before.
You eat with a disbelieving zest

busy in the heat of remembering.
You're immersed in a comical
misery that belongs to a very long time ago:
it must have been of importance once.
You bite; it tastes alive again.

Tunnel

The remnants of salad swim in the trough.
Entering at ten past seven,
you sense plenty's retreat.
In the furnace glow
of the hot food counter,
where, last week, you chose
a burrito lifeless
as a bandicoot, now
you point to a smudged triangle
of pizza dimpled with pepperoni.
As backup, you've banked
a bowl with couscous and a submerged layer of coleslaw.
You eat alone;
always, excess
is conjoined with impoverishment. Nothing
adds up. You pile more food.
The pizza is skin; you're sure
the fragments can be pieced together
into an anatomy
but find somehow you're at the end of it all,
the tunnel into which accumulations vanish.

Salt and Vinegar

I consumed the salt and vinegar crisps
in a single gulp.
The packet ballooned with volume
to greet me; a twin
of my stomach, but darker –
when I finished
it wasn't as empty as my stomach once had been,
my hand stretched further into it
like a glove
and came up with shards, jagged
in the depths, the world's splintered residue.

Zombies

These four,
dumped
on the manicured shore of Eastern
Australia, are sheepish
as they struggle into uniforms
for the 'cook'.
Neither convict nor indentured
labour, not migrant or
native, they're ever-smiling,
sacrificial homebodies
coastline-sequestered
with access to every abundance –
shiitake mushrooms;
John Dory; anaesthetised soft-shell crab;
blow torches and blast chillers
(everything they've handled with the inborn
propriety of Picassos and children) – now
there's panic, like they're on
a liner in sight of an iceberg.
They scurry from imminent wreckage.
Tomatoes drop from hands; the cooker refuses
to catch flame – the floor shifts.
'Plate up, plate up!' The cry ripples inward.
They're coming! Suddenly you spot them.
The zombies!
Forty or fifty of them. Their serene,
irrevocable, end-of-the-world
progress ceases at the table.
Here they sit, gazing expressionlessly, as if
unaware of the passing of years. They will wait
forever, unexpectedly peaceful.
The would-be chefs are

never prepared for them, their work's
unfinished, their defences bare.
The zombies look neither deterred nor urgent.

Chalta

Woman's an animal with language.
When she pushes the *chaltar ambal*
toward me
I view the green soup
with scepticism.
She confesses: 'I have it to chew
the *chalta*' –
whereas, I
reserve my mouth to swallow words
hardly ever putting my teeth to use.
She, though, can issue
such articulations and immediately
forget them as she destroys
the rind to make
the juice she ruminates over on her tongue.

Sandesh mould

Furtive as a sea horse
or something
that's danced underwater
to a current
outside time and light
to survive
as residue –
one a brooch, another
as corpse
of fish or mango,
yet another
with the submerged finality
of a seal,
each form
shakes itself free
to swim away – are you
then cradle or
exoskeleton:
are you finished, or about to begin?

Orange Juice Concentrate

Orange juice concentrate
I had
in 1973
in a crystalline land.
I know now
it wasn't juice at all
but pale gasoline
to scour throats
and oesophagi
of an unprecedented machinery.
You didn't think of oranges
when drinking it; in fact,
you didn't drink it any more
than a machine swigging
down oil drinks fire; tasting nothing
but the habit of replenishment.

They

They would come
from Chandannagar
the thumb-sized
patol, man's creation, not
nature's, the
stony custard apples.
Near them
the karhais,
spatulas,
child-size, possessed
by an over-reigning normalcy.
Satisfying no hunger
but of seeing –
the dissociated gaze's
appetite for existence.

Yesterday

Deep in the bowel of the earth
(as they say)
where it was boiling
standing once alone, once with my daughter
I noticed the Piccadilly Line's withering
over time
the way a humerus thinned
by polio
dangles in space, barely glanced at
except extensions at Heathrow
and Hounslow, phalanges
redundant but oddly firmer.

Oxford

You know
it's two minutes away
but it takes about ten
to get in.
The train
slows down
in the night
and Oxford moves toward you
pushing
in the opposite direction; inside,
there is stoic concentration and
disbelief in these last inexplicable
moments, as if
the journey had drifted
into an iceberg
and motion
were being absorbed and buried.
Oxford looms.
It can't be seen.
With each moment
it pulverises arrival.

St Cyril Road

Into which language should I translate you
now you're gone?
And how to find that reader?
Not in the lane itself, where nothing but a moonstruck
cottage stands in daylight, windows shut.
It keeps its secrets.
The 'reader' can't walk in these lines,
can't stare or pause. Buildings
spring up everywhere like icicles.
Bougainvillaea
is a word that always had the texture of something
artificial, like papier-mâché.
I don't remember if it was 'real'.
My poem was hardly ever visited
but you were discovered too often.
I'm sad I no longer want to describe you.

Shireen

Dipping a straw
into the submarine past
I sip through Apple music
a song embarrassingly peripheral
when I was twelve
which I listen to, Shireen,
because, 'one floor below me
you don't even know me',
I realise we've still hardly spoken to each other
except that once, in Bombay,
I called for your brother's number
when my daughter developed an allergic cough.
In school, they made us miserable
and hostile by launching
into the wretched song if you crossed my path.
I discover that Tony Orlando *could* sing.
Your father's recreational violin-playing
ascended the window of the eleventh floor
and who know what noises *I* made.
A flash of sea; separate worlds;
in those worlds, separate vigils
kept for love and tomorrow, with no thought
of heeding the knock when it would come.

The Fake and the Organic

There's a kind of person
who goes to Fabindia
wearing a Fabindia kurta.
Whether the choice was predetermined
or whether, as on reaching a country
you find you're standing out
due to an unexpected familiarity,
there's an intuition, in this person
– as he weaves past the piled-up clothes –
of proprietorship and disinheritance,
of possessing what he'd come to seek,
thereby possessing nothing.
You belong here, like an edict,
flows into *You've been caught out*
as if he'd overstated
tell-tale signs of the fake and the organic.

Biros

Sometimes I let them lie
at an angle to one another.
I view the two with equal patronage.

In India, I watch them splay
like sticks, or harden like straws,
a whole bunch I've gathered from a walk,
still, uprooted,
with a hint of the old murmuring.

Apartment

Like a labourer
stooping
in the odour
of work
or a fishmonger's pores
admitting without hindrance
the smell of scales
every being
in the apartment
lives blind
on the oxygen
of chicken curry
for days.
It's irrevocably
in the towel –
burnt cinnamon sticks,
turmeric,
garlic, and onions – as in a shallow
of breath, the soft
perspiring cloth
pressing damply on the face.

Leaving Paris

I depart
in less than thirty days.
For months
I've dispensed
this washing liquid –
thick globules –
because it lathers so poorly –
yet there's more.
Today I see the sub-text:
'Ecologique'.
Massive as snot
as when the head-cold recedes
our daily encounters
have become a race with time
to see
who runs out first.

Three

The Story of My Life

I'm trying to read
the story of my life.
It's already written.
Only, the language
is unfamiliar.
Mostly, it's hidden from me,
this story, because of the way my hand crouches
on the page, or grasps
another hand, or an object –
it's lost in companionableness
and discreet sensation.
If I glance at it, it's to
acknowledge the back, which is
like the cover of a closed volume.
The fingers inevitably curl and fence
off a secret. Only when I turn
and lay it flat does a narrative
appear, plain and illuminated.
Summaries
of delays and departures,
outcomes and botched-up plans
engraved on a parchment,
the etching
of lifelong attachment –
the palm shrinks periodically, like a lotus.
There's no apparent distinction between
what's finished and unfinished.
The story's composed
of gradients
devolving a journey's beginning and petering out,
or cuneiform hieroglyphs
legible only to dead men.

I stare at it. Every postulate
and episode seems a scar.
Every word in the language has meaning.
The story's there. It's been written.
I experience it without being able to read it.

The Reader

I wrote poems not for you
but presumed you'd be the reader.
Even now, these lines form
concomitant with your unknown
make-up, flesh, and DNA.
Writing is a kind of hope
as much as growing old is.
Did you grow old? Did you cross
the finishing line of youth? Are you
by chance no more? Was it
your remains I saw
the other day?
Are you, like bone, reduced
to facets of bare truth?

Reading *Kaddish*

Reading *Kaddish*
after my cousin's death
I see mothers heal
even when they're fearful and mad.
Naomi is anarchic and scared
of the world – when she implodes, it's messy.
Allen is the crutch; or he thinks so.
He's full of pity and exasperation.
All the time, she remains his mother.
In this, she does what mothers do –
saves him, and envelopes him
with herself. Allen feels nothing but love.

Rereading those lines last night
for some reason on hearing my cousin died
I think of my mother in St Cyril Road
nudging me when a maidservant
who worked for her, face disfigured
by burns, would be reunited with her children.
We would ignore her, because the remnants
of the face hit us hard, but, 'See,'
my mother would say, of the two
who dropped by on the way home from school,
'for them their horror-mother is everything.'
For two minutes we'd be amused
by the not-so-strange, but strange, context of their excitement.

Kaddish, last night you taught me that
no mother can be terrible
or ugly or angry or threatening
however it seems to the onlooker.
Always, there's peace at the proximity
and certainty of the embrace.

Reading Li Shangyin on Emirates while listening to Joni Mitchell

I bypass the dragons.
The wind's tremulous.
Suddenly there's a hush
between one valley and another.
If the sun ascends a second time
after the first
will it mean day has dawned on the world?
This sound – wail of farewell
and yearning – hum of the wind –
voice in my ear – my attention lapses
momentarily – the voice says
nothing; only moans
with a reminiscent calm, cuts through the grass
from the world's edge; a thousand years later
in my immediate past
it trickles into
the ruins of poems in my hands.

Sighs, unknowing, on the alien alphabet:
('O my love, my darling,
I've hungered for your touch'.)

The Pleistocene Epoch

To you the question came
in Norfolk or North London
gripped by the remnants
of icy sunlight –
of whether 'the Pleistocene Epoch itself
has come to an end'.

For me, and others
who have inherited the earth
the question is suspended. I stare out of the window
of this college room
at what can only be called
premeditated shrubbery
and note the absolute reign
of sunlight in that theatre
I once knew as a student.
A new era's at hand.

I never dreamt the day would come
when I'd ask for dark
to envelop the shrubbery:
at night, I feel its presence
but morning reassigns its place to it again.

Prynne, your life
inhabited the rim
of mine. Yet there was
obvious overlap:
we wake to the same day
yet this is where the trip
you started long ago
nears its destination;

you barely see
the sun rising on this world;
I'm stirred,
reading you,
by my immensity of loss.

Keith Jarrett

That grunting –
is it singing?
Or an overlay of breath
that's mostly silent
but, in the transport of playing,
becomes rasping and tuneless?
I find I'm listening less
to the magic keys
than the passionate noise of his singalong.
I'm nervous, as I would
be about some homeless commuter
on the NYC subway
who's keeping time, shaking, oblivious
to humanity, the music all in their head.
Or does that frenzied shout
have nothing to do with anything at all –
effort; exhaustion; determination
to keep it going for another second –
like the tennis player lifting their body to serve?

Vinyl

Not the music
was the memory
but the loud scratching
at the start –
a plunge
into the realm of noise
before it becomes
melody, noise skirting silence.
The ear picked it up, and forgot
the undertone of a period –
this is what it meant
to live then on the verge, a signal
absent now – our children
needn't encounter it –
this expunging just when we begin.

Sybille Bedford

A Legacy's in Classics.
One copy on the first floor.
A crystal
wedged between
Beckett and somebody else. No one
knows it's there. If it's prised out
from its lodging, the structure
will come down. *Jigsaw*

is sundered from *A Legacy*
exiled
to General Travel Writing
in the basement, though
it's fiction. Near-invisible
on the shelf. Like
a princess in a story, it waits.
Whoever goes to it
a year from now
is seeking
no other. Descending
to Travel, he'll ask
for General Travel Writing. He's
no hero, but the one the book
waited to meet in time
and space, in given material form.
At his touch, it starts
from its featureless vigil.

Blackface

Not so easy
to shed white skin,
Laurence Olivier!
You need
the luck
of forefathers
with unimpeded sun.
Then one day
you'll notice
as Africans did
five hundred years ago
the light absorbed
has transformed
into a surface
of dark gold.

Buskers

Carfax is a cross
formed by
High Street, Queen Street,
Cornmarket Street, St Aldate's.
From the apocalyptic verge
I turn
to Marks and Spencer's – there
an earnest man
in black jeans
is telling a boy
without let up about Jesus.
I hear the word 'Christ'.
Nothing else.
Standing on one plank of the cross
at Carfax
he addresses the teenager
with soft urgency.

The buskers
on adjacent
Cornmarket Street
stand or sit a few feet apart
occupying
distinct universes.

Sometimes people encircle one and cheer.
Sometimes a girl will stop and stare.

On Cornmarket Street
they become their own tomorrow.

The audience
is an exception for those who sing.
All who play and dance
are doing it for themselves
in a haze. They cry
from a private sorrow. Listeners
loiter from morning to sundown
like walkers on a beach. A man
cradles his guitar in an alley
by the Crown, inaccessible,
like a temple carving.
                              Buskers –
Tagore with his 'song offerings'.
Flinging them in the direction
of anyone, letting them land anywhere.

Tuchchho Kobita

I like the word 'tuchchho'.
It contains its pride.
Its insubstantiality
opposes its true being.
What it states
is what it tastes
of: a fleeting sweetness.
How can what's
tuchchho be homeless?
It's always close, like an only
child. We never beget epics.

Poem

Dreaming of Shakti Chattopadhyay
or a line that may not at all be his
I wake up
not with the newborn's sudden
anticipation of day
but a terminal patient's awareness
of pointlessness.
With English, I was on loan,
a parcel whose addressee had moved
and couldn't be returned to sender.
What can I do with a language
which is mine no more than my body
or any worldly possession?
Will it come of use
when I'm with God
or my mother?
Better to have been a drunken baul
vanishing obstreperously from city to village
and leaving no trace but words.

Poem

The aftermath of euphoria
is the image
each image
being a body-part
pulsing separately
like a parasite;
this is what stays –
the truncating
into thighs, bellies, the anguished curves
of organs
seeking repose.
Pornography! If only
you'd had your Goya
to capture the revolutionary
battlefield before the conflict
became rehearsed
and bodies grew cold.

To a Poem

Where were you?
Three weeks went
and I missed you not knowing it.
Always the fear,
the speculation,
illogical, plausible,
of not finding you again.
Even now, I'm not sure
it's you who are returning
to my life. But anticipation's
already made you possible, and
possibility brings joy.

Untitled

A poem's journey
isn't made to a clock.
Even if you date it
you have no idea
how to disentangle
its coming
from its departure.
Is whatever it is
that follows birth
an aftermath
– what humans call 'life' –
or does a poem
have no future, no later?
Kolatkar felt
a millennium may have passed
in its approach –
as with a ray from a star.
We are, by then, certainly dead.
How can
we comprehend its language
with no grasp
of its calendar?
Why are we convinced
it was meant for us?

Crazed

We're crazed
even when we don't know it.
Our movements
are journeys
tracing a circuit –
we're aware
of this; more often, we're not,
but spring madly
like houseflies
I encountered late in the morning
in the drawing room,
dancing over the carpet, sparks
behind the light flashing off the glass
table, not knowing
the rules of the dance, but madly
considering each possibility.

Daphne

Running, you become leaf
so you can't be
possessed by man or god.
Your subsequent
stillness, your fragile
defencelessness confuses him.

Now you desire the opposite.
You want closeness
when there's none.
So you're a figurine
in a drawing room, a deity
meant to be polished, not worshipped.
To be ignored
is to breathe his breath and smell him
without his permission.
The stone marked by a smudge
beneath the tree,
the money plant,
the fly's frustration on the glass:
all these are you
in various moods and times of day.
Invisible and near.

Death-Song

Having been called
to sing
at an auditorium
where music
will indent
the obituary, I speculate
whom I will sing to.
Is it you, absent one
whom I knew in person hardly –
your smile floats
away; it's the only
thing that escapes you – or
is it the living
who gather to take in the song?
Not quite music, it's something else
wrenched from situation and whatever life-
experience gave birth to melody.
It's not intended to survive.
It dies to engender.

Timekeeper

See him –
whatever frenzy possesses
the hands and arms
his face is humane, distant;
a somnolent kindness defines him
where he sits bent
stoical before the onslaught
that electrifies the others.
Invisible figure of sanity,
he can't go mad, because
he keeps time.
So Clark Pierson
in those last days
witnesses the conflagration
of Janis.
So Charlie Watts
waited and waited
journeying, not moving an inch,
as Jagger was unsprung
by marijuana and the market.
He saw him without looking at him;
he looked at him without seeing him.
And saw everything.

Four

Daybreak 1st January

From light's margin
comes your coughing.
I grasp sleep. Awash, I cherish
and resist your closeness. You
shudder gently, supine.
I hear the repeated pairs –
cough, cough; cough, cough;
the glue of sleep competes
with the longevity
of sound, breath, all we know –
cough, cough. You are life –
life, loyally, has woken us,
though, curled up, we pretend
we're root; as unrelated
as bodies are, parallel
and horizontal, are the disruptions
of declamations; bird-cry.
I embrace them, since they're mine
as much as your cough is mine
to receive and yours to release
then let them go and surrender
this spasm of breath and love
to what of course we have no memory of.

Post-Midnight, Rain

It's not 'sound'
but low-pitched white noise.
Onset of silence
that wasn't there
a second ago
underneath
the swing
and abrupt intake of breath
of air conditioning,
the memory
of machinery –
the overhead fan,
quiet as a bird
flying in the dark –
behind these, an absence,
absolute and brief.

Evening, 2nd October 2019

It's warm, fuzzy,
and still.
Everything's
waiting for something.
The fan,
with open arms,
flings the anjali
of breeze.
It rains marigold
where I sit
hunched
like a child
at obeisance.

Dhak

On the eighth day at six o' clock. On the ninth day at seven. Roughly thirty seconds. Approaching with what must only be merriment. I don't open my eyes; I smile in half-sleep.

The tattoo not just sacred, but comic. *They're so funny, all of them*, I think, of the living dhaki and his assistant and the fictional entourage. Takta-tatak – takta-tatak: impossible to take seriously. It's intrusive, sweetly mocking, like a finger. A mother's smile when you fall. You get up, teeter forward. Takta-tatak, it says; and is gone. You hear it the rest of the day, like your cellphone when it's on silent. You don't find it in temple or court. It's the fag-end of a fairy tale.

Five

Parents

Will I see them one day
like a young soldier who's returned
home after a war
he thought would never end,
entering the hush of the drawing room
to find them sitting there?

Mother

'Mother' was simply one of you –
with that funny nose
the freckled tip,
your exacting littleness.
The manifold stick-on teep on the forehead.
You were a singer.
From diaphragm up and down
you were music: clear, surprising tone.
I feel now I'd encountered you
at other times – 'force of nature' is said
glibly of many, and was only part-true of you.
I would have recognised you in forms
immaterial, material, human and
old and insentient; prescient, I saw
you before knowing it was you,
and, retrospective, in the aftermath,
found you again, even when I didn't
know you, I knew you were before me;
'mother' was only one of you –
that printed silk sari, the low-heeled sandals –
you were multiple, too diverse,
for me not to have, in this world and others,
forgotten you, fallen into your presence.

Radha, Before Term

All day she's sat in bed
laptop parted before her
like a book planted on its side
legs for hours submerged
in the quilt's blue interior –
mermaid-like
she keeps vigil
waiting maybe for no one.

At night, switching the light off
I see her face brightened
as by a hurricane lamp
eyes shining
while she looks to the horizon.

Block C

What's this building
pastel blue-white
deep modern stone
immovable,
windows throwing light sharply
during day,
reticent at night?
B's separated from C
by prehistoric water
shallow in summer
demarcated by a concrete ledge.
In it, brutalist lines
shimmer
with a vibration
that's smothered periodically
by geese;
otherwise, calm
settles on that façade
that flutters like a pennant
in a faint breeze.

The Squid and the Whale

When they separate
they become
their own people once more
with unwanted charge of their destinies.
That's how the child sees it.
Furtively, he watches them cross the street
away from him and each other
as if they're young again.
He'll learn to fend for himself,
however old he might be.

So with death. Then too
they part. They'll find their way
and possibly find new names.
They can't be the child's any more
though the child is always theirs.
They've grown restless; their future
is their deepest prerogative.
He suddenly realises they're gone.

Wind-Up

'Baba!
You're listening to Celine Dion!'
I'd turned the volume up
to hear the warbling
over the shower.
'Research,' I said.
She fled the scene.
                    I think
she'd have
taken any explanation.

The truth is
I saw no harm
in slipping
three into the phone.
'My Heart Will Go On' which
I attend to
for the fake lifting of the key.
'That's The Way It Is'
I've masticated on
repeatedly
like chewing gum.
The less said of my
annual curiosity
for 'A New Day
Has Come' the better.

                    Yesterday,
she pried again: 'Baba,
don't you listen to Madonna?'
'Only three songs.'

'"American Pie",' she said. 'Yes,
and "Beautiful Stranger"…
The third…
the name escapes me.
It's the clever faux country song.'
I swipe my phone.
'"Don't Tell Me".' 'Why
won't you listen to her other stuff?'
'I don't like it.'
My daughter and I then
put these questions
to one side.

Perfect

I have it on my phone now.
She doesn't need to know.
Often she calls me 'Mr Bean'
but now and then
I find her meditating
on the puzzle I evidently am.
What drew me to Celine Dion?
That question's losing
its incandescence.
But *him* – I used to call him Ned,
enquiring if his face was pasted
to his glasses, bristled at the blank
eyes above the smile. Then, the other day,
like a waiter who takes a sip from one
of the glasses he's carrying, closing his eyes
and cancelling the room, I downloaded
the song. It's on my phone.
Given her final
indifference
to what I do
I suspect she'll put it down
to being 'my business'.

Thresholds

She could never take heat
on her palate
but now
I see her add
chilli oil
without comment –
inadvertent, practicable.
Her calmness
throws me
as her teenage fits once did.
I started at the other pole:
my mother boasting
my first diet was shutki,
four years old
weeping, sniffing, belching,
wanting more.
Of my daughter
I've wondered
given her generation's
innocence
of thresholds
what it'll take
to accept
that burning –
is the tongue somehow learning –
the chilli oil
a silent riyaaz
whose notes will
sound freely?

Onward Motion

What's this onward motion
this current –
where are we going,
me, my daughter;
tomorrow, where will she be?
I walk
up Linton Road
unobstructed
to the room
in which she's enveloped.
There's a backward motion too
imperceptible –
in the underground
when I stepped onto
the escalator
grasping the handrail
which fell behind me
while I sought it
with my hand –
steadying myself
as on a gondola
pushing forward.

Eating at Home

The more my daughter eats out
the more it feels food at home
has got better. When did we last taste
this extraordinariness at a stretch?
My mother's no longer alive.
Even when she was, I can't remember
such an uninterrupted and unthreatened
phase, when the seasoning
and spices were
unimprovable, the out-of-season jackfruit
and chhana full of auburn colour a return
to existence; the bhetki fried
in parcels of pumpkin leaves
has a freshness that can't derive from ingredients alone.

For visitors my wife brought out
a pot of tamarind chutney
made when my mother was there.
The coarse gur-coated chhara was hair
unspooling from an atavistic scalp
that in time grew
sweet-sour: we eat our forebears.
I'm sure about nothing. I can't say
how long it will last, or if we're
in an era with no justification.
Something is being given
to us in a middle period in which
our lives are changed but we are not,
my parents have receded, we are guests at home,
our bodies work (we possess them fully);
our daughter, grown, is semi-absent –
I wonder if she'll stay unmindful of this food
in her experience of winter – will
the cook leave us one day, as my parents did?

Life-line

For my father in law

Randomly promoted
to business class
I lie recumbent
on being airborne.
My feet go into a cavern.
I lose my shoes.
Prostrate, I weigh memories:
they come, unheralded,
between images on the screen.
At this altitude, they have
no history.
I can't judge
which is older – walking
down Park Street, or waking
next to you early this morning.
I'm ill.
Sunk in comfort, I stare
at the filaments
of my life-lines:
the charger's cord; the remote control's
shoelace-thick wire;
the unentangled reel
to my headphones.
They drip, drip, drip
life into my horizontal body
or do I eke into
them the resistance I'd hoarded?
A small light I haven't seen before
is keeping vigil above.

Our Parents

How embarrassing they are!
Some of their views
can be extraordinary.
Increasingly, we were torn
between protecting and
disowning them
for at least fifteen minutes.
In the end, when they left,
it had little to do with us.
They don't stick to a plan.
On one level, so focused
on organising our lives,
on another, as it turns out,
unreliable in their departure.

The Laws of Physics and Gravity

The laws of physics and gravity
are defied by the sheep of Scotland.
However the earth jolts from back
to stomach, the sheep are unmoved,
fixed on green hills, untouched
by the convulsions of day and night.
Like stars they are, steadily glowing
against the skin of darkness.
So much emptiness and speed
between the stars – but see, everything else
plummets, except the stars
grazing on infinity.

Six

Short Q and A

Q. How do you know if you're an experimental film-maker?

A. If, after decades of making cinema and receiving acclaim and honours, the Damocles of uncertainty hangs on you as you begin your new film just as it did when you'd made your first, if there is no guarantee that it will be shown in cinemas or even seen, you can conclude with some certainty that you're an experimental filmmaker.

Q. Who or what is a poet?

A. A poet is a religious figure. That is to say, the voice of the poet can't be heard. This leads to the purity of the line.

Q. Who or what are men?

A. Men are those who create and break the laws.

Q. Who or what is a human?

A. A human is one who can bear infinite pain.

Q. What is an endorsement?

A. An endorsement is the death of championing.

Q. What do the words 'the people' mean?

A. They are a justification for any and every action. But Mandelstam uses them without justification when he claims 'The people need poetry that will be their own secret/ to keep them awake forever'.

Q. What excites a writer most?

A. Making another poem.

Q. What's to be made of J, the Indian critic who has no compunctions about writing forewords and essays on any writer, artist, or filmmaker, notwithstanding what he feels about them, for money?

A. Well, he insists on getting paid. There's no shortage of people who do the same for nothing.

Q. In what way are you different from Mr Bean?

A. He detests Charlie Chaplin.

Q. What causes most distress in a writer's legacy?

A. Their 'politics'. Far from causing revulsion, bad writing is hardly noticed.

Q. What might be an instance of a back-handed compliment?

A. 'I admire your optimism.'

Q. What's the difference between a writer's work and their reputation?

A. A writer's work provokes envy or calculated indifference; elicits admiration or a desire to emulate. A writer's reputation is wedded to legitimacy. It's why we ask for endorsements from writers we may have never read and may never read.

Q. Who or what is a racist?

A. Someone who believes in human values for people with their own set of features. A woman standing in a queue, making baby-sounds to an infant, glowered when she saw me. Selective humanity undermines more than terror.

Q. How might a person of colour temporarily hold off a violent racist?

A. By laughing at his racist jokes.

Q. Why would he laugh at racist jokes?

A. To stave off an attack and (as no one can fake such responses) because he found them funny.

Q. Why would he find them funny?

A. Because every intelligent person feels moments of disgust towards his own community, and a joke relieves that anger.

Q. When would someone say, 'Take out your penis'?

A. In a rushed preamble to lovemaking.

Q. When else?

A. In a different kind of emergency, to check if you're Muslim or Jewish.

Q. Which answer is ok for the first but not for the second?

A. 'I'll show you mine if you show me yours.'

Q. Why is 'Hit the Road Jack' so short?

A. Because life makes no sense.

Q. What is an instance of a fundamental desire that is realisable and has been set aside through forgetfulness?

A. When I was a boy, I dreamed of having a beard. I thought today, 'I've always been clean-shaven.'

Q. What's your top priority when you're in the West?

A. To finish the dishes.

Q. What do managers manage?

A. The imagination. Before them, it ran wild.

Q. Why does the writing feel tired when you write for too long?

A. Because the imagination is a muscle.

Q. What is required to maintain an acceptable standard of morality?

A. A scapegoat.

Q. Who is impossible to sentimentalise?

A. Your mother, as she's the first being in whom you learn to love imperfection.

Q. What is 'savouring'?

A. A return to life. You're reunited with the quotidian. You savour its taste without constraint.

Q. Why is there a shortage of mental health institutions to 'normalise' aberrant behaviour?

A. The task of 'normalisation' has passed to universities and corporations.

Q. What's the difference between playing a part on the stage and playing one in 'real life'?

A. The actor is unmindful of their audience.

Q. Can you have a true sense of sorrow if you live in extraordinary privilege?

A. Think of Gautama.

Q. What is an archive?

A. The past.

Q. What is poetry?

A. A form of subtraction where words are viewed as impediments.

Q. Who might we say led a life of privilege?

A. Walter Benjamin.

Q. What is privilege?

A. Privilege is what fails to protect us.

Q. What is the worst thing about American winters?

A. Wearing thermals in a heated room.

Q. What's the difference between epic theatre and realist theatre?

A. Epic theatre gives to us for the hundredth time a story we know. We have even memorised its lines. Realist theatre gives us a 'new' story that confirms the conventions we're schooled in. We go to epic theatre for the already known. We go to realist theatre for the expected.

Q. Which question have you been asking yourself lately?

A. 'I wonder if I'll miss Amy Robbins?'

Q. Who is Amy Robbins?

A. Someone who disapproves of me intellectually, and whom I hope never to run into after two months.

Q. Why are you wondering if you'll miss her?

A. Because, although it's hard to love everyone, it's possible to miss anyone or anything.

Q. Define a particular spiritual need.

A. The desire to not understand at once.

Q. Was this what Pound meant when he wished for *The Waste Land* a not 'single and unique success'?

A. Hard to be sure.

Q. When Eliot called Pound 'il miglior fabbro', did he mean Pound had imparted some clarity to his poem?

A. Unlikely.

Q. Why is craft spiritual?

A. Because it devises ways to conceal meaning.

Q. Does concealing meaning require craft?

A. Yes. It's near-impossible to speak without meaning something.

Q. Name a difference between summer and winter.

A. Smells move faster in summer, sounds in the winter.

Q. What's another name for the future?

A. The past. It's where you encounter yourself.

Q. The future has already happened?

A. No. But you'll recognise neighbourhoods you're still to visit.

Q. What is value?

A. Value is a kind of understanding that comes when ties are loosened. It's a piece of music whose beauty you for some reason ignored most of your life.

Q. What is research?

A. Research is what you've learnt from past lives. Your memory of it is vague, but it gives you an affinity for certain lived concepts.

Q. Who are a saint's first followers?

A. His teachers. They are his first audience.

Q. Who asks the questions?

A. This is information I can't share with you.

Notes

1. Srinivasa Ramanujan (1887–1920) was an Indian mathematician whose work came to the attention of the mathematician G. H. Hardy after Ramanujan wrote to him. Ramanujan was invited to Cambridge by Hardy, and lived in England from 1914–19. He then returned to India, where he lived until his death in 1920.

2. Papworth Hospital was founded in 1918 as a sanatorium for discharged soldiers with tuberculosis. Ramanujan spent some time there after he was diagnosed with TB. It later became a centre for heart disease.

3. Srirangapatna, in Karnataka, was the capital of Mysore under Tipu Sultan. It's where Tipu fell in a key battle against the British in 1799, with historic consequences for Empire.

4. The Campus Kitchen is at the University of East Anglia.

5. Shakti Chattopadhyay (1933–95) was a Bengali poet.

6. 'the Pleistocene Epoch itself/ has come to an end': from J. H. Prynne's 'The Glacial Question, Unsolved'.

7. 'Tuchchho', in Bengali, means 'insignificant' or 'inconsequential'.

Lightning Source UK Ltd.
Milton Keynes UK
UKHW010715260521
384398UK00001B/39

9 781848 617384